How to use this book

Follow the advice, in italics, given for teachers on each page.
***Praise** the children at every step!*

Detailed guidance is provided in the Read Write Inc. Phonics Handbook

8 reading activities

Children:

- *Practise reading the speed sounds.*
- *Read the green and red words for the story.*
- *Listen as you read the introduction.*
- *Discuss the vocabulary check with you.*
- *Read the story.*
- *Re-read the story and discuss the 'questions to talk about'.*
- *Re-read the story with fluency and expression.*
- *Practise reading the speed words.*

Speed sounds

Consonants *Say the pure sounds (do not add 'uh').*

f ff	l ll	m	n	r	s	v **ve** (circled)	z s	sh	th	ng nk

b	c k ck	d	g	h	j	p	qu	t	w wh	x	y	**ch** (circled) tch

Vowels *Say the sounds in and out of order.*

at	hen	in	on	up	day	see	high	blow	zoo

*Each box contains one sound but sometimes more than one grapheme. Focus graphemes are **circled**.*

Green words

Read in Fred Talk (sounds).

big bag had got have

Read the root word first and then with the ending.

chip → chips

lot → lots

Red words

I said of no

Vocabulary check

Discuss the meaning (as used in the story) after the children have read the word.

	definition:
chips	*long bits of potato fried in oil (mmmm!)*

Punctuation to note in this story:

Sam Kim Tim Jen	*Capital letter for names*
Can But Yes	*Capital letters that start sentences*
.	*Full stop at the end of each sentence.*
!	*Exclamation mark used to show anger and surprise*
?	*Question mark*

Chips

Introduction

I love eating chips from a fish and chip shop out of a paper bag. Have you ever done this?

In this story, a little girl called Kim sits on a seat outside a chip shop with her bag of chips. Three friends come up to her and demand a chip, one after the other, but they all take large handfuls.

You can guess what happens at the end!

Story written by Gill Munton
Illustrated by Tim Archbold

Kim had a big bag of chips.

"Can I have a chip?" said Sam.

"Yes," said Kim.

But Sam got *lots* of chips!

"Can I have a chip?" said Jen.

"Yes," said Kim.

But Jen got *lots* of chips!

"Can I have a chip?" said Tim.

"Yes," said Kim.

But Tim got *lots* of chips!

Kim had a big bag ...

but no chips!

Questions to talk about

FIND IT QUESTIONS

✓ *Turn to the page*

✓ *Read the question to the children*

✓ *Find the answer*

Page 8:	*What is Kim thinking about as she sits with her bag of chips?*
Page 9:	*How do we know that Sam is impolite?*
Page 10:	*How do we know that Jen is impolite?*
Page 11:	*How do we know that Tim is impolite?*
Page 12-13:	*What is Kim feeling now?* *(angry / frustrated / cross / disappointed / hungry)*